DATE DUE			

870318

585
BRO

Brown, Anne Ensign.

Monarchs of the
forest.

MONARCHS
of the
FOREST

MONARCHS
of the
FOREST

The Story of the Redwoods

Anne Ensign Brown
Illustrated with photographs and drawings

DODD, MEAD & COMPANY
New York

Illustration Credits

Anne Ensign Brown, page 10, 27, 32 (top right), 46, 48, 65 (left); Joseph E. Brown, 2, 14 (top right), 14 (bottom), 20, 23, 25, 29, 32 (left), 36, 65 (right), 69; David H. Swanlund, 6, 14 (top left), 17, 28, 30, 32 (bottom right), 39, 42, 51, 57, 86, 87, 88, 91, 92; from the Collection of David H. Swanlund, 77, 78, 79, 81.

For Mom and Dad who love the forest

1   2   3   4   5   6   7   8   9   10

Library of Congress Cataloging in Publication Data

Brown, Anne Ensign.
Monarchs of the forest.

Includes index.
Summary: Discusses the three species of redwood trees,
which now grow naturally only in California, Oregon, and
China.
1. Redwood—Juvenile literature.   2. Giant sequoia—
Juvenile literature.   3. Dawn redwood—Juvenile
literature.   4. Forests and forestry—California—
Juvenile literature.   5. Forest ecology—California—
Juvenile literature.   [1. Redwood.   2. Giant sequoia.
3. Dawn redwood.   4. Forest ecology]   I. Title.
QK494.5.T3B76   1984   585'.2   84-1535
ISBN 0-396-08322-6

Contents

Redwoods are the tallest trees on earth. This is the Rockefeller Grove in Redwood National Park.

Foreword

Redwoods are the largest, tallest, and among the longest-living things on earth. Members of the conifer or cone-bearing family of trees, they were on earth at least 130 million years ago, ranking them among the earliest of trees. They once were found over vast areas of the globe. Today, the three species of redwoods grow naturally only in California, in a small tip of southwestern Oregon, and in a section of China.

Coast redwoods may reach an age of 2,200 years, and one of their number is the tallest tree in the world. The giant sequoia of California's Sierra Nevada range is the oldest living of the three species, sometimes attaining an age of 3,600 years. Only the much smaller bristlecone pine, which reaches 4,000 years or more, lives longer.

To visit a redwood forest is to experience awe, perhaps even reverence, not only because of the great age and size of these lofty monarchs, but also because of their great hardiness. Throughout the centuries, these trees have endured the assault of storms, fire, strong winds, and disease.

The term "cathedral-like" is often used to describe the feeling in a dense redwood grove. The term is appropriate. The grove appears dark and hushed. In forests of the coastal species, it is damp and misty and it is this mist—the product of coastal fog—which is so necessary to the tree's growth.

The first humans to see the redwoods were probably the ancestors of today's Indians—bands of hunters, fishermen, and food gatherers who roamed across present-day North America perhaps 10,000 years ago. The white man did not arrive on the West Coast until the sixteenth century. Today, the redwoods grow in a region which has become one of the most populous in America.

Although the redwoods' range has diminished through the millennia, it was not many years ago that the trees in the present range numbered in the millions. That number has been drastically reduced, due in part to encroachment of human populations and to logging practices.

Although there have been many attempts to "save the redwoods," it was not until 1902 that groves in California's Big Basin, south of San Francisco, were set aside by public law for future generations to enjoy.

Since then, public-spirited citizens and conservation groups have worked hard to develop a system of state parks and two national parks to save these mighty trees.

Here, humans may come to contemplate living things which were growing when their own civilization was only beginning, hundreds of human generations ago.

Drawing representing the Jurassic period when redwoods flourished. Small dinosaur is a Comsognathus. Birds are Dimorphoden and Rhamphorhynchus. Plants are ginkgoes and cycads.

1

Ancient Immortal

If we could look back on time some 130 million years ago during the Upper Jurassic period of dinosaurs, giant ferns, and winged lizards, only one living thing would appear familiar out of a myriad of plant and animal species—the redwood tree. The redwoods existing today are the only surviving remnants of that ancient world, a splendid race of needled giants from an era long past.

Through millions of years these giants stood, the lone needled trees among enormous bizarre ferns, cycads, and ginkgoes. However, during the Cretaceous and into the Tertiary periods of some 60 million years duration, many of these strange ancient plants, along with the unusual animals of the time, slowly disappeared and other needle- and cone-laden trees arrived to join the redwood.

These trees, so similar to the redwood, are conifers, an order of trees to which the redwood also belongs. The trees of this order all produce cones that carry the tree's seeds. Their tall, straight trunks are of a soft wood. Most of these conifers are also known as evergreens because they retain their green needlelike leaves year round. By shedding their leaves in a rotating manner, all are replaced at least every few years.

Conifers were the first trees in the plant kingdom, the redwood being the very first. These various conifers formed the dominant type of forest 100 million years ago.

Hardwood trees such as oak, cherry, maple, and walnut soon began to grow among the conifers, and together these forests thrived for millions of years.

By the beginning of the Miocene epoch, 25 million years ago, what we call the "Redwood Empire" spanned the Northern Hemisphere from Western Canada to the Atlantic and from France to Japan. Along with fossils found throughout Europe, redwood fossils have turned up in the now frozen barren lands of Greenland, the arctic islands, Alaska, and St. Lawrence Island in the Bering Sea. At least a dozen redwood species that existed during the so-called "Age of Conifers" have been identified from fossils.

Around the close of the Miocene epoch, the earth's climate began cooling and drying. This continued for several million years, and as this occurred the redwoods began to retreat. Then, approximately one million years ago, the cooling became radical. The Ice Age had taken over and the remaining trees were reduced to the small areas that remain today.

In the arctic, frozen glaciers swept over dense forests. As these glaciers moved steadily south, the great forests of what is now Europe succumbed, losing nearly all their native species. In what is now Asia, the story was the same: only a few remaining survivors. In the territory we now call America, the number of species was drastically reduced and the redwood species that remained had a very limited range.

With the southward glacial movement, earthquakes, and volcanic eruptions, the American Redwood Empire of several species that had spanned a large area of at least ten states was reduced to two species in two relatively small separate areas of California and southwest Oregon.

The giant sequoia, *Sequoiadendron giganteum*, grows in isolated groves of the Sierra Nevada. Along a narrow coastal strip of northern California stands the coast redwood, *Sequoia sempervirens*.

There are a number of differences between the two sequoias, even though they are closely related. Their habitats are quite different. The coast redwood thrives in the misty coastal atmosphere of summer fog and winter rains, while the giant withstands the snow and dry, clear air of the high inland Sierra region. The coast redwoods cluster together on both hill slopes and streamside flats, while the giants grow in more open stands. The coast redwood is taller, more slender, and relatively younger than the shorter, stockier giant. Though both species have reddish bark, it differs considerably, and their bough pattern and distribution of needles and cones also differ.

LEFT: *A giant sequoia—the General Grant Tree.* RIGHT: *Coast redwoods in the Muir Woods*

Close-up of a dawn redwood

The third species of redwood is one of the few conifer survivors of Asia. The dawn redwood (*Metasequoia glyptostroboides*) was only recently discovered in central China. There, the temperature and humidity had remained just right, enabling its survival. In 1944 one of these dawn redwoods, a species thought dead for millions of years, was found growing. It is the only remaining Asian redwood species. Soon, several hundred more of these trees were located. A species of tree that once populated forests from the Black Sea to Greenland now is found only in one small region of the Szechwan and Hupei provinces.

Before the sequoias were classified, they were merely called redwoods because of the hue of their bark. Both the wood and the bark of these trees are reddish in color, particularly in the coast redwood.

The first record of these trees was found in the journal of Fray Juan Crespi, a Franciscan missionary who was accompanying the Spanish explorer Portola on his 1769 expedition from Baja California to the Monterey area. The first botanical examination of redwoods was started in 1794 when Archibald Menzies, a Scottish botanist, collected foliage, cones, and seeds of the coast redwood trees and took them to the Natural History Museum of London for study. However, it was not scientifically named until 1824 when the English botanist A. B. Lambert placed the redwood in the genus *Taxodium* of the cypress or Taxodiaccae family and added the name *sempervirens* ("ever-living") because of the tree's ability to generate sprouts from its base.

Stephen Endlicher, an Austrian botanist, disagreed with Lambert's placing the redwood in the *Taxodium* genus and proposed a new genus name, *Sequoia*. It is thought that Endlicher's great admiration for Sequoyah, an American half-breed Cherokee Indian, inspired the name for this native American tree.

But the battle of the botanists over the redwood name had only just begun.

In 1852, A. T. Dowd discovered one of the two groves of giant sequoias in Calaveras County, California, and sent specimens to Albert Kellogg at the San Francisco Academy of Sciences for study. Three years later, he and his colleague D. H. Behr assigned the name *Taxodium giganteum* to the Sierra redwood, completely ignoring Endlicher's designation of the genus *Sequoia*.

In 1853, English naturalist William Lobb, on seeing Kellogg's samples, left immediately for the Calaveras grove to gather his own cones, seeds, and foliage. Lobb showed these to the noted English botanist John Lindley who, in turn, published the first official name in an article describing the tree in *Gardner's Chronicle* of December, 1853. In this description he called the tree *Wellingtonia gigantea* in honor of the Duke of Wellington because "the California tree towers above the forest as Wellington towers above his contemporaries."

Infuriated by the British name for an American tree, American botanists retaliated with *Taxodium washingtonianum* and *Washingtonia californica*.

Apparently not wanting to be left out, French botanist Joseph

The Calaveras grove today

Decaisne declared that both were wrong. Rather than nationalistic designations, a botanically accurate name would be more fitting. Since both the coast and the Sierra redwoods belonged to the same genus, Endlicher's term *Sequoia* was more appropriate. Perhaps this may have been just a subtle way of doing away with *Wellingtonia*, the British name honoring the man who did away with France's Napoleon at Waterloo. Decaisne, however, did retain Lindley's *gigantea* as the species name.

Later, in 1938, botanist John Buchholz noted many differences between the coast and Sierra trees. He then proposed the scientific name *Sequoiadendron giganteum* for the Sierra trees, which was officially accepted.

Thus the names *Sequoia sempervirens*, ever-living sequoia, for the coast redwood, and *Sequoiadendron giganteum*, for the giant redwood of the Sierra, came about. The third species, the Asian dawn redwood, is classified *Metasequoia glyptostroboides* to distinguish it from the two true Sequoia redwoods.

Today as one wanders through a redwood grove, the sense of time is felt overwhelmingly. The essence of the past in relation to the future is caught in the touch of an ancient living tree, and the centuries it has known; or in the glimpse of a nearby, new sprout, and the centuries it will know.

In these forests is one of life's most fascinating stories.

2

Kings of the Coast

A tiny redwood seed nestles among the fallen needles of the damp forest floor. Though smaller than a ladybug, this minute seed contains a determined life force that may one day enable it to become one of the world's tallest living things.

Its aging parent, the *Sequoia sempervirens* or coast redwood, stands a few feet away. One of the statuesque monarchs of the forest, its crown of branches reaches some 350 feet into the sky. About the time this ancient tree was only a tiny seed, Christ was born in Bethlehem, Augustus reigned as the first Roman emperor, and in China a new monarch seized the throne to begin the Hsin dynasty.

This frail seed of 2,000 years ago had been one of the few to survive. Of the thousands of seeds which fell from the small,

A coast redwood

acorn-sized cones of the parent tree, only a third or so were capable of growing and developing. Not only did this particular seed have the spark of life, but also it was carried by a gentle breeze to a perfect spot on the forest floor where the dew-laden soil and the soft light could nurture it.

After the splitting of its thin shell, a tiny root from the seed went down into the warm, damp soil, and a fragile sprout rose into the air.

Growing steadily, the tender seedling soon became a promising sapling. Straight and graceful, a filigree of silver and green foliage wreathed its amber-hued trunk as it reached high into the light.

A fine net of shallow root tentacles soon spread out beneath the earth reaching for water and minerals—the tree's life-sustaining nutrients.

Deep inside the tree's trunk, the xylem or sapwood layers carried water and minerals from the roots to the leaves and stored up some of the nutrients as a reserve supply. As the sapwood aged and died, the transport process ceased and these woody layers became the heartwood, the tree's strength. Though dead, the heartwood would stand sturdily as long as the cells around it continued to be nourished.

In the cambium, the next layer out, production of the new, continually dividing cells added more new layers.

The phloem or inner bark, the next layer, took over the dead sapwood's role of transporting and storing the nutrients.

The rich, reddish brown outer layer, from which the redwood

takes its name, protected these vital inner layers. When sunlight reached the matter in the tree's leaves that provided for their green color, called chlorophyll, carbohydrates were formed by the conversion of water the tree soaked up. Carbohydrates consist of carbon, hydrogen, and oxygen, and in turn, through a process called photosynthesis, produced the nourishment the tree needed to grow.

The redwood's age is no secret; the trunk's heartwood reveals a precise growth record. The rings seen in a cut log or stump show the tree's annual growth. The dark outside edges of the rings are the summer growth of small cells, and the light inner part is the spring growth of the larger, less dense cells. Each year a new band of red heartwood surrounds the old, forming another ring.

The sapling's trunk gradually filled out and grew tall. It had lost its early fir tree appearance of soft lacy sprays of green and silver foliage from base to tip. As the trunk reached upward, it shed its lower, tender foliage. Garlands of needled boughs, appearing high up the new pillar, tapered to a majestic crown. If one could have seen inside to the heartwood, nearly 300 rings would have been revealed.

During those first few centuries, the tree endured many of the hazards of growing up. It survived assault from insects, birds, and rodents in its seedling years. It withstood bear and porcupine attacks as a sapling. Through the centuries it continued to grow, despite fires from lightning, wind storms of hurricane force and the accompanying danger of being crushed by neighboring wind-toppled giants.

A fallen redwood

The hazards did not cease. A great mass movement of rain clouds spiraled eastward over the sea toward the northern California coast. Upon meeting with the atmosphere of the coastal mountain ranges, these clouds loosed a deluge of rain, swelling the banks of the rivers.

When at last the clouds had spent themselves and the sun once more shed its light on the forest floor, only a desolate expanse of

23

thick silt and debris was exposed. The lush greens of ferns and oxalis and the rainbow colors of flowers and berries lay devastated several feet below.

The silt had a suffocating effect on the redwoods, for their roots must lie near the surface in order to reach their life-giving nutrients. Now the roots lay several feet deep. However, the hardiness for survival and growth with which nature had endowed this tree had not been buried. Soon a new and higher root system developed to absorb the needed nutrients. Slowly the damage was rectified and the tree recovered sufficiently.

The tree's lofty branches rose higher, continuing to produce new seed cones year after year, while battling nature's capricious ways.

One unusually hot dry summer was followed by a cold dry winter, only to be succeeded by more fogless summers and rainless winters which seared the already parched forests. The forest greens turned to desert browns, and the smell of ozone was in the static air as a flash of lightning struck the dry foliage which crackled and snapped as it ignited the dry undergrowth, kindling the vulnerable old monarch above. The flames licked up the red protective bark like so much tinder. But on reaching the inner bark, the dampness of the water transport and storage system was sufficient to eventually smother the flames. The tree was saved, but not before fire had burned deep into the inner bark, leaving a gaping, blackened wound. As the decades passed, new tissue and new bark healed the wound but a telltale scar was left to tell the story.

Old age is inevitable to all, even to the *Sequoia sempervirens,*

24

*Close-up of a coast redwood
hollowed out by fire*

and the hazards continued. Though more vulnerable than in its youth, the tree endured. Many centuries later, one particularly bad fire licked deep into the heartwood of one side of the tree, also killing the roots on that side and causing the straight old monarch to lean on the injured side.

Now almost 1,900 years old, the tree seemed doomed, but it had one final defense: a crutch. Almost imperceptibly the old giant had still been adding growth. That growth temporarily nearly ceased, as all its efforts were put into building its crutch or buttress. Year by year the support grew until another century had passed and the buttress projected out several feet to support the crippled monarch. Disfigured though it was, it continued to produce new seeds.

Now in the twentieth century, death will come soon, perhaps in a windstorm as the leaning tree, heavy with wind in its boughs, will give way in the rain-sodden soil and crash to the earth.

However, even in death the old monarch will not be defeated. As spring comes, fresh shoots will rise from the severed roots and detached burls of the fallen monarch. These new shoots are not a new generation like the sprout from a seed, but the same life, a continuation of the ancient tree, still surviving—ever-living sequoia.

This cycle of life will continue to repeat itself just as it has for centuries. It begins each year between November and March when tiny male and female conelets are produced on different branches of the same tree. In May, pollination usually occurs when winds blow sulphur-colored pollen from the male cone to the female cone. Approximately five months later, the female cone will be mature enough to produce the tiny 1/16-inch-long seeds. Of the thousands of seeds that fall, only a third of these will sprout and reach the seedling stage. Even as a seedling, life is precarious. Only one in every one million seedlings survives to become a sapling. Of these survivors, some may grow into trees weighing 500 tons and may even exceed 367 feet, the height of the tallest known tree in the world. This tree called simply Tall Tree grows in a grove near

Seed dispersal of a coast redwood. TOP: *Male and female coast redwood cones. Wind blows pollen from male to female cones where the sperm from the male cones fertilizes the female eggs.* SECOND: *The female matures into a tight rounded cone that produces the tree's seeds.* THIRD: *Cone loosens and opens up as it develops.* BOTTOM: *Finally it opens up enough to release the seeds.*

Leaves and cones of a coast redwood

California's Pacific Coast in what is now Redwood National Park.

Sprouting is the second way in which these monarchs reproduce. It results from the activation of a bud which has been temporarily dormant. An injury to the parent tree stimulates the bud into sprouting. Large woody masses of these buds form burls of a beautiful, intricate wood grain on the trunks of redwoods. Sometimes, an entire trunk may sprout, forming a ring of new trees around the injured tree, giving rise to the term "cathedral trees."

Another exceptional characteristic of the redwoods is its extreme hardiness. No known diseases will kill mature *sempervirens*, nor do any insects severely damage them after the seedling stage. Fire, though a definite danger to seedlings, seldom seriously damages or destroys the almost fire-tolerant mature tree due to a lack of flammable resins, which fuel fire in other species. A fire in a redwood forest can actually be a blessing. As the underbrush and fire-vulnerable species succumb to the flames, the duff or humus layer of the forest floor burns off, leaving a mineral seedbed where redwood seedlings can flourish again.

The domain of these trees is a 450-mile-long strip along the northern coast of California. The range extends naturally from southwestern Oregon's Chetco River south to Salmon Creek in Monterey County, California. This narrow belt averages some 30 miles in width and covers approximately 2 million acres (10 percent of which remains in old growth or virgin redwoods).

Coast redwood burls. These are about twelve to fourteen inches in diameter.

Coast redwood country

Underlying much of the northern California coast are rocks known as the Franciscan Assemblage. These rocks consist of muddy sandstones, conglomerates, and volcanics formed from 70 million years of river rocks and sediments washing onto the sea floor, mixing with rocks of the oceanic crust, the continental crust, and earth's mantle.

About 160 million years ago, when the Pacific's eastern sea floor "collided" with the edge of the North American continent, the accumulation of sediments rose to form the Franciscan Assemblage, the present Coast range mountains. This range rises from sea level to an altitude of 3,097 feet and has a varied topography. In some places there are gently rounded summits, in others steep-sided slopes. Along the coast there are marine terraces, sand and rock beaches with offshore sea stacks (jagged rock islets), lagoons, and sandbars. Beach cliffs are of deposited river sediments in some areas and of older Franciscan bedrock in others.

The climate of this redwood domain is temperate and moist— mild wet winters and moderately dry summers.

Most important to the coast redwood is fog, a low cloud layer caused by the marine influence. Fog moderates even the area's hottest, driest summer conditions. Redwoods lose hundreds of gallons of water through transpiration in only one hot, dry day. By condensing on the foliage and dripping to the ground, coastal fog helps to reduce this water loss.

These loftiest of all living things truly are the "kings of their race," as the famed naturalist John Muir called them. Forming a darkened cathedral-like forest, they dominate a wealth of plant and animal species.

Ferns, a common plant in the redwood forest

Oxalis ground cover

Coast redwood and associated trees in the Muir Woods, California

3

The Coastal Forest Community

In size, the Douglas fir is the redwood's closest rival, although even its large column of light brown bark, wreathed in aromatic needled boughs, is dwarfed by the coast redwood. Other trees in the redwood region include the tanoak, western hemlock, and madrona. Along the streams are the big-leaf maple and near the coast are stands of Sitka spruce.

Beneath these forest trees several species of fern spread their lacy leaves, veiling small bleeding hearts, oxalis (redwood sorrel), wild ginger, redwood violet, and countless herbs. Flowering shrubs and berries include the California huckleberry, dogwood, azalea, and a proliferation of pink rhododendron.

Shrews in search of prey hide among the greenery and blossoms of the forest floor. Douglas squirrels, or chickaree, leap from tree to tree, pausing now and then to nibble a seed cone. Western gray squirrels search the tanoaks for acorns and fungi. Black bear, elk, deer, mountain lion, bobcat, and coyote also prowl these verdant forests.

Along the silt flats, the melodious notes of the varied thrush and winter wrens contrast with the harsh scolding of Stellar jays and ravens.

However, it is not the flora and fauna of the magnificent dense redwood stands alone that are important but also the ecological features of the entire forest complex of rivers, streams, estuaries, woods, prairies, and seacoast so delicately interwoven to form this redwood domain.

Here mountain streams trickle down to join the tidal creeks and large rivers which eventually reach the edge of the sea, rising and falling with the salty tidewaters, creating an estuary.

At times, waves rush in from far out at sea, rising high, claiming the land for its own, inundating reeds, grasses, and sodden meadowlands to form brackish marshes and lagoons. These are the interlocking waterways that provide homes for a wide variety of wildlife species.

Let's take a look and see what we may find here. In summertime near the mouths of rivers and streams, spotted sandpipers can be seen teetering about the edges, as a fun-loving river otter splashes and slides in the mud. Upstream a beaver diligently cuts a tunnel into the bank for its winter home. The evenings hum with the sounds of insects in the air. A water ouzel, a strange bird, walks underwater on the stream's bottom, looking for aquatic insects. A great blue heron stands poised to strike an unsuspecting frog or salamander. A raccoon approaches the water's edge in anticipation of a crayfish dinner. Belted kingfishers and osprey keep a silent vigil for small trout or silver alevin from their perches in the branches high above the stream. King or Chinook salmon can be seen on their summer spawning run.

After the first frost, icy waters reflect the brilliant, golden reds and browns of big-leaf and vine maples in autumn attire. Rivers and streams are a flurry of activity as trout begin their autumn-winter spawning run. It is time, too, for the king and silver or coho salmon to spawn in the many shallow streams and tributaries.

With the coming of winter, the streams and rivers of the red-wood region swell, rising so high that the moss-covered maple trees, willows, and laurel crowding the riverbanks in summer will be bent and torn under torrents of rushing water.

Spring announces itself in an array of pastel colors. Streams, creeks, and pools now reflect the pinks, blues, and whites of azaleas, blueblossom, and dogwood. Skunk cabbage scents the air, and orange salmon berries and yellow redwood violets are mirrored in the quiet stream pools.

Dotting the dense forests like little islands in the sea are the prairies or meadowlands—small expanses of grassy, treeless space where wildlife abounds. In spring, the wild flowers here are a celebration of color. As spring fades so do its bright blossoms. Only the lush greens of summer grass remain. In its turn the green will

35

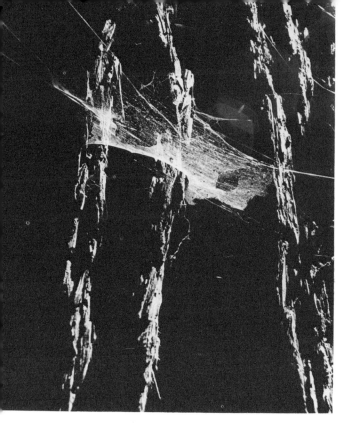

Spider web on a coast redwood

mellow to gold and amber as the summer dew crystallizes to autumn frosts.

Prairies are scattered throughout the coast redwood domain. They are found both near the shore and farther inland, on slopes as well as in the flats. Usually there is a wooded edge of oak, madrona, laurel, big-leaf maple, and Douglas fir around the inland prairies, while red alder and Sitka spruce rim the coastal prairie lands.

The exact conditions that created and maintained the prairies are not known. It is known, however, that the prairies are usually underlaid by soils that differ from nearby forest soils. Fire may also be a factor in prairie maintenance.

Native American Indians sometimes burned away the dry leaves to make it easier to collect acorns in the oak woodlands at the prairie's edge. Burning also stimulated Indian potato and hazel, prized for basket material. Soon the Indians found that burning produced a new variety of forage for deer and elk, making easier hunting as these animals came into the open to feed. Later, European settlers used the prairies for pasture and cultivation.

The prairie is one of the redwood domain's most prolific wildlife habitats. Swallows in search of insects skim the tall waving grasses. Chickadees dangle from twigs at the forest's edge in search of seeds and berries. Hummingbirds, juncos, and birds of prey find picking here easier than in the hiding places of the dense forest. Meadowlarks and quail dart in and out among the tall blades.

Most imposing are the Roosevelt elk. Once widely distributed in California from Mount Shasta to the Central Valley, they can still be found in a couple of areas of the coast redwood domain. Other prairie mammals include deer, bear, fox, coyote, raccoon, and porcupine.

In contrast to the misty primeval stillness of the forest, the gentle quiet of rippling streams, and the whisper of wind through the prairie grass, the seacoast can be a din of thundering surf on the rocky shore, wailing winter winds, and wheeling gulls.

Yet at times this same seacoast can be hauntingly still in a summer fog, muting even the gentle lap of an ebbing tide.

A massive semipermanent weather system called the Pacific High is primarily the cause of this coastal atmosphere. In spring and summer, the high pressure dominates atmospheric circulation, and winds are generally northwesterly. In early fall the high weakens and is pushed about by stronger low-pressure systems that come from the Gulf of Alaska. These shifting high and low pressure areas control the various patterns of rainfall, ocean winds and waves, and fog.

The California Current also exerts its influence on the coast. Though this cool current has very little seasonal temperature fluctuation, its position shifts slightly, due to the movement of the pressure systems. As it moves, it brings rich nutrients up from the ocean depths, providing a food supply for many organisms.

Past the surf, seals and sea lions search for fish and crustaceans. Commonest of these are the giant Stellar sea lions, the playful California sea lion, and the harbor seal.

Offshore spouts mark the presence of California gray whales, migrating between the Bering Sea and Baja California in Mexico. Dolphins and killer whales also cruise these waters.

Many seabirds soar gracefully high above the ocean. By far the most common are gulls. The brown pelican is a summer visitor and the cormorants frequent the lagoon and shore waters. Shorebirds in the redwood seacoast region are oyster catchers, willet, black turnstones, and sanderlings.

Between the sea and the low expanse of grass, reeds, and half-submerged meadowlands lie the seastacks, saltings, and tidal pools

The Prairie Creek area of the Redwood National Park

of the intertidal zone, a habitat for varied plants and animals. Beneath the surface can be seen a kaleidoscope of pattern and color, reflecting many bright, living treasures of the tide pools and tidal channels.

Where the shore begins to slope upward, coastal shrubs, coyote brush, silk tassel, current, blueblossom, and salal are prolific. The vegetation intermixes with coastal prairie and coastal forest flora, forming a patchwork of many types of plants. Here and there among the varied grasses, California blackberry and sword fern grow in a tangle. Spring bursts forth with purple lupine, larkspur, thistle, white daisies, and yellow mustard.

Song sparrows, wren-tit, Bewick's wrens, and red-tailed hawks feed in the protection of these slopes.

Sculptured by the wind, odd-shaped Sitka spruce and alder forests, tolerant of the strong ocean winds and salt air, act as a buffer and shelter for the shallow-rooted coast redwood forest just beyond.

This harmonious plant and animal life of forest, prairie, and shore form a true *climax community*, the natural balance of an ecosystem formed over a long period of time which has been undisturbed by extreme natural disaster or human impact. Overall, more than 1,000 species of flora and fauna inhabit the coastal redwood domain, including several rare and endangered species: California gray whales, bald eagles, brown pelicans, peregrine falcons, and the Aleutian form of the Canada goose.

A climax community is rare anywhere today, but it is particularly surprising to find this Utopia of nature in populous California.

4

The Mountain Giants

Far inland from the domain of the coast redwood, a smoky blue haze rises from the Sierra foothills. Storm clouds shroud the highlands above, softly frosting a layer of crystal white on the gray sculptured granite of the Sierra Nevada. The haze rises higher, swirling upward past pine and firs above the slatelike ridges, enveloping the crowns of the massive giant sequoias—largest trees on earth.

It is midwinter in the Sierras as tiny male cones, covering the outer foliage of the upper branches, send amber pollen adrift on the mountain breezes, tinting the snow below.

At the time of pollination by the male cones, the female cones on the same tree are only about the size of a grain of wheat. As the summer nears, the developing female cones begin to produce

41

Cone of the sequoia redwood

chlorophyll which colors them a bright green, their winged seeds a light straw color. By the end of the first growing season, they will have reached three-fourths of their full size.

When the female seed-bearing cones reach maturity, they will be about 2.5 inches long and 1.75 inches in width, with an average of 34 cone scales covering their egg shape. Each cone scale produces from four to seven seeds, and each average cone produces approximately 200 seeds.

Unlike the cones of the coast redwood and most other conifers, these neither turn brown nor release their seeds of their own accord at maturity. They remain green, changing their hue slightly and increasing in size each year. The vascular connections, or channels, between the cones and their seeds remain intact until released and dispersed by acts of nature.

The age of a sequoia cone can be determined by counting the annual growth rings in a cross-section of a cut cone, just as one determines the age of the tree itself.

About 1,500 to 2,000 new cones are produced in a normal year. A large sequoia tree at any given time might contain approximately 11,000 cones, of which 7,000 would be closed, fleshy, and photosynthetically active. The remaining ones are open, brown, and seedless. Cone production can occur on trees as young as ten years old and may continue after 3,000 years of age.

Approximately 400,000 seeds are released from each mature tree per year. With an average of three mature trees per acre, more than one million seeds are produced annually per acre per year in most groves.

Since the cones don't automatically release the seeds at maturity, how are these seeds dispersed? A high percentage are released by animal activities.

Tiny Douglas squirrels or chickarees dart from tree to tree, feeding on the seeds of pines, firs, and the fleshy green scales of the young sequoia cones. This "master forester of the mountains," as John Muir once called it, strips the flesh from the outer portions of the scales, dislodging the tiny seeds of the giant sequoia as it feeds, scattering the uneaten ones literally by the millions to the leaf-litter below.

The chickaree also cuts off thousands of green cones each year. When the cones are dropped and it has had its fill of the seeds, the chickaree then stores the rest of the cones for winter. It buries them by the hundreds and thousands in the damp duff of the forest floor to feast again on its return in late fall and winter. Later, as the chickaree feeds at each of these storage places, it spills more seeds in these widely scattered caches, again contributing to the sequoia's potential regeneration.

During the years of low population, the squirrels are less aggressive. They store fewer cones and eat more of the cones' seeds in the trees as they are found. As many of the seeds fall, they are caught on the autumn breezes, spilling them in a rain. Their small, oval wings ride the breeze sometimes as far as 600 feet from the parent tree. Some of these spilled seeds will germinate in the spring, producing a frail seedling.

Another forest creature that helps in the regeneration of the giant sequoia is the tiny, long-horned, wood-boring beetle *Phymatodes nitidus*.

The female beetle lays her eggs in among the cone scales. Upon hatching, the larvae chew their way into the interior of the cone for nourishment. Often during this feeding process the vascular system of the cone is severed, cutting off the water supply to the ends of the cone scales. This causes them to dry out and turn brown. The scales then shrink, creating gaps between them, slowly allowing for the dispersal of the seeds.

Eight of these little beetles might feed in a single cone. About one-quarter to one-third of the cones in an average tree brown and disperse seeds due to the work of these beetles.

Chickarees seem to prefer cones between two and five years of age, while the beetles prefer cones four years old or older, so competition between the two species is no real problem.

Fire, wind, and snow storms also contribute to seed release, but not to the extent of animal activities.

The seeds of the world's largest trees are quite small. At maturity, most are one-eighth to one-fourth inch in length and only three-quarters of that in width. Between the straw-colored wings lies the tiny embryo.

Loose mineral soil is best for the germination of the sequoia seeds. It must be disturbed in some way to bury the seeds. Nature does this in several ways: avalanches, floods, and fire. Fire is the most important of these. As it burns away the organic content of the uppermost layer of the soil, temporary spaces are left between the particles. Falling from the crown, the seeds are buried about one-quarter inch deep in these spaces. Protection from the drying sun, enough moisture and minerals from the soil, and a compatible temperature to insure germination are provided by the spaces. Proper temperature and soil moisture conditions for seedling survival are best in spring.

Because of the small amount of food stored in sequoia seeds, the

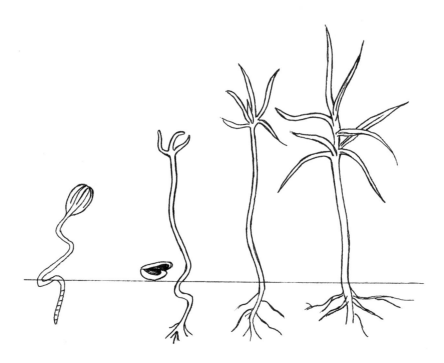

Developmental stages of the giant sequoia (left to right): seedling still in shell, shell has popped off, embryonic leaves begin to spread out, secondary leaves forming at center.

newly germinated seedlings must become rapidly self-sufficient. Often the beginning stages of germination occur beneath the snow, and the seedling roots are as much as two inches long before the snow melts.

As soon as the protective seed coat is shed from the new tender shoot, an adequate root system must be able to supply the seedling with the necessities for photosynthesis.

The most frequent cause of seedling death is the drying out of the soil. Other causes are burial by falling leaves, root fungi, and damage by insect, bird, and mammal.

For the giant sequoia seedling to thrive the soil condition must be somewhere between the two extremes of open/dry and shaded/moist. If the soil is too dry, the seedling will reach a permanent wilting point and die. If the soil is too moist, fungi, root rot, gray mold blight, and other disease agents may bring about the seedling's death.

Seedlings grow best in full sunlight with a light layer of leaf-litter covering the soil. The risk of seedlings dying from the heat is highest during the first few weeks after seed germination. By the seedling's third year, its root system is more than a foot in length and can penetrate the soil to a level beneath the midsummer dryness.

Another hazard to seedlings is death by shading. Sequoias are very vulnerable to low light intensity. If they survive in a very shaded area at all, they will grow twisted and undersized.

Survival of seedlings is tenuous. John Muir estimated that not one seed in one million germinates and that not one seedling in 10,000 attains maturity. These may not be exact figures, but frailty of the sequoia in these early stages is no myth.

A full-grown sequoia that you see today would have been a fledgling in the Bronze Age. That tree would now be approaching 4,000 years of age. This living giant might stand approximately 300 feet high and be 30 feet in diameter. In this same forest, there are hundreds of trees from 2,500 to 3,500 years old and thousands

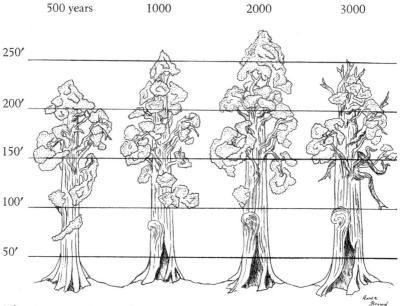

The giant sequoia at various ages

of 1,500-year-olds, along with 10,000 or so tiny new seedlings. Possibly some of these may live on for the next 4,000 years to surpass today's oldest living sequoia.

The new emerging sequoia seedling is only one inch high at the time the seed coat is shed. There are three to six seed leaves having a bright green surface with a reddish underside. The juvenile leaves begin to appear within a few weeks as little rosettes in the centers of the seed cones. Within two to ten weeks the seed leaves wilt and fall away. By late summer branching begins, and by autumn the seedling may have as many as six little branches on its three- to four-inch trunk. The leaves at this time are linear and taper to a fine point like that of the adult sequoia. The root system has also branched out with a taproot four or five inches long, which it will later lose completely.

During the second year, if conditions are favorable, the seedling may grow a foot in height and display the lovely oval crown of foliage that distinguishes the giant sequoia.

Growth rates of young sequoias vary considerably, depending on seed distribution and on survival of the new seedlings. Competition increases with density. In time, thinning out occurs naturally as the crowns and roots expand and compete for light and water, the weaker dying out.

The seedlings that survive develop a narrow conical spire, assuring that the sun will reach part of each crown in the dense stands. These trees are now saplings and their sharp, pointed crowns may continue to grow for a hundred years or more, reaching up to heights of 150 feet. The branches, slightly ascended, are dense with a lush green foliage with green seed-bearing cones tucked among the boughs.

The root system at this stage has spread out laterally and the taproot is now reduced. The taproot seldom reaches more than three feet in depth before reduction begins, eventually completely disappearing, but the lateral root system spread may reach out to a hundred feet.

Trees at this stage, if in the open, may have branches all the way to the ground like a Christmas tree, but trees that are shaded will loose their lower branches and the crown will begin a half or third the way up the trunk.

49

As the giant sequoia ages, the brownish-gray scales of the bark begin to slough away, exposing the cinnamon red for which the tree was named.

This red bark is quite thick, thicker than on any other living tree, and is a major factor in the tree's longevity. As the tree grows outward, the bark splits vertically. In several hundred-year-old trees, these bark ridges average about ten inches in thickness, with some sections measuring up to two feet thick. Trees of intermediate age seem to have the thickest bark, with trunk diameters of eight to twelve feet. As the tree continues to age, the slough-off of the bark scales tends to increase.

At about 600 years of age, the vertical growth slows in comparison to the growth of the lateral limbs. The crown has attained the rounded shape which generally is considered the mark of a mature tree. However, the rounded tops of many mature trees have been altered due to fire. When fire penetrates through the bark and vital inner layers, disrupting water and mineral flow to the crown, the rounded top dies back.

Mature tree trunks may be ten to twenty feet in diameter. Height of mature Sierran trees varies with site quality and the degree of fire damage at the base. Trees in the bottomlands generally attain greater heights. The tallest known giant sequoias are about 310 feet.

Trunks are usually bare for 100 to 150 feet. On the well-known General Sherman Tree, the largest living thing, the biggest limb is 130 feet from the ground. Its diameter is seven feet and curves

The General Sherman Tree

outward to approximately 125 feet. This branch alone is larger than most whole trees of other species.

The area size of the mature sequoia's root system varies with the availability of soil moisture. Roots may extend only 50 feet from the trunk's base in moist drainage bottoms, but where the soil is well drained roots may reach out as far as 125 feet. Roots tend to grow in a generally circular pattern around the tree, often covering an acre. The number of small terminal roots branching out in all directions is important to sequoia growth. The upper two feet of soil are a tangle of these roots, which dwindle rapidly in number below this depth. Individual roots may occasionally reach down to a depth of five feet in extremely dry areas.

The wood of these mature giants is brittle, making up in bulk what it lacks in strength. This brittleness may well have been the salvation of these ancient sequoias as lumbering interest turned to species of a stronger nature.

The giant sequoia is generally resistant to fire and rot. The amount of tannin it contains is considered to be the reason for the great fire resistance of its bark. The dried wood of the brittle upper limbs is of a lower tannin content and has virtually no resin so is much more vulnerable to fire, as well as rot.

The longevity of the giant sequoias is almost as famed as their size. These largest of all living things are in age second only to the bristlecone pine.

Sequoias generally die by toppling caused by fire, extreme weight for their shallow roots, water-softened soil, wind, root rot, snow load, stream undercutting, falling neighboring trees, and carpenter ant damage, or combinations of these causes.

Even in death these ancient giants continue to play their role in nature. As the sapwood of the giant trunk decays, the nutrients are released into the soil to nurture tiny new seedlings, insuring the persistence of this incredible species.

5

The Sierra Forest
Community

Like most living things, the giant sequoia does not live alone. It is one of a complex interaction of plants and animals, and its survival depends on the interdependence of ecological and living factors.

Each organism has its role within a community or ecosystem. Beginning the sequence in the energy chain are the green plants, the producers. The animals that derive their sustenance from plants, known as herbivores, are the primary consumers. Animals that feed on other animals, or carnivores, are secondary consumers. In the sequoia communities the giant sequoia is one of the main producers, the chickaree a primary consumer, feeding on the sequoia cones, and the marten a secondary consumer preying on the chickarees.

The individuals of the community interact along these food

chains, one form of life feeding upon another. The chains are rarely isolated from one another. Each link or consumer may feed on more than one organism, thus interweaving the chains to form complex food webs. This is the reason the elimination of any species of the community or link in the chain can disrupt the balance of nature and cause the whole web to fall apart.

In an ecosystem energy flows only one way and is used up, but nutrients can be used over and over again.

Through photosynthesis, the giant sequoia captures energy and uses it to maintain itself and supply two food webs as well. One web of consumers feeds directly upon the tree itself. The other is a web of organisms which decompose the dead parts of the tree, such as fungi and insects. The giant sequoia and its decomposers are probably in balance because the soil around these ancient trees is not yet depleted of nutrients. This is due to the constant decomposition of branches, needles, and cones as the decomposers industriously return the nutrients to the soil.

Factors such as temperature and soil moisture are important to survival of a species. The degree of change in temperature and moisture will determine population distribution, size, and even survival of each organism.

Though these physical factors generally determine which individuals can flourish in a certain area, it is possible for an individual to alter the area as well. If an individual of a certain community brings about conditions detrimental to a member species, the intolerant species may be eliminated and succeeded by a new species which finds these same conditions favorable. This is termed plant succession, and the phenomenon can also come about after a major disturbance such as flood or fire where the ecosystem is altered and certain species may not be able to adapt to the new conditions.

The sequoia community is canopied by the lofty crowns of the giants, along with umbrellas of sugar pine and ponderosa pine; white, red, and Douglas fir; and incense cedar shading the younger, smaller pine and fir; California black, live, and canyon oak. Shrubs of mountain whitehorn, chinquapin, California hazelnuts, and Pacific dogwood intermingle.

The ground cover of the heavily shaded floor is rich and varies from grove to grove. Dwarfed at the feet of the giants nestle trail plant, sweet cicely, white hawkweed, wood violet, larkspur, buttercup, wild strawberry, and a forest of tiny white fir seedlings.

In the fire-disturbed areas delicate gilia, popcorn flowers, primrose, and gooseberries pop up to hide the blackened earth with a carpet of rainbow colors.

Along the streamsides of the sequoia groves in spring are the lovely white blossoms of the western azaleas, which in fall again brighten the forest with reddish foliage. In spring, bracken fern and bright purple lupine color the flood plains and gentle slopes.

As in other communities, vertebrate populations of the Sierras vary with location, season, food supply, and other necessities of life. However, the mixed conifers of the sequoia community support a wealth of animal life, much of it present throughout the Sierras year round.

Mariposa redwoods and museum, Sequoia National Park, California

Bird populations are a striking feature of these groves. The most abundant are the yellow-rumped warbler, western tanager, mountain chickadee, brown creeper, Oregon junco, nuthatch, Stellar jay, and the golden-crowned kinglet. Several species of hawks and owls also live in these forests. The dominance of one species over another varies with the stage of plant succession.

Mammals are also populous but are not seen easily because of their shyness and nocturnal habits. Most common are the deer mouse, gray squirrel, Douglas squirrel, golden-mantled squirrel, California ground squirrel, mule deer, coyote, black bear, and many species of gregarious chipmunk. Seldom seen are the shyer Trowbredge shrew, bobcat, marten, weasel, and mountain lion.

Populations of shrews, moles, mice, gophers, and raccoons can be found throughout the riparian communities of the Sierran conifers.

In foliage, cones, trees, and old dwellings hide the many and varied bat species.

A wide variety of small lizards, snakes, toads, frogs, and salamanders also have their role in this complex ecosystem.

Even smaller, but just as important, is the myriad of invertebrates. Except for nineteen species of insects, little is recorded of the many other invertebrates. These tiny creatures, too, are important links in the communities' complex food web, sometimes even more important to the giant sequoia than their larger forest neighbors. The long-horned beetle, which plays such an important role in the reproductive life of the giant sequoia, is but one of the many beetles, moths, wasps, ants, flies, lice, larvae, and aphids which in some way interact with the sequoia. These tiny invertebrates and their role coacting with the even tinier fungi and bacteria of this forest ecosystem are not to be overlooked in this land of the giants.

The sequoia line has been traced as far back as the Jurassic period. However, redwood ancestors of these date back as far as the Devonian time—some 300 million years ago.

Sequoia reichenbachii and *Sequoia couttsiae* are the earliest close relatives of the giant sequoia. Fossils of these are found through much of the Northern Hemisphere in the Cretaceous and Tertiary rocks of such diverse places as Greenland, Alaska, Canada, and England. Though closely related, their morphology differs enough to indicate that they are not its immediate ancestors. The most direct ancestor to the living giant sequoia dates some 10 to 20 million years back to the Miocene epoch in Idaho.

The most recent North American fossils of presumed direct lineage with the giants were discovered at Trapper Creek in southern Idaho. These fossils, called *Sequoiadendron chaneyi*, lived about 400 miles northeast of the living groves of the Sierra Nevada in California. Other fossils have been found in four separate areas within 100 miles of Reno, Nevada, placing the ancient range closer to that of today's stands.

Today's giant sequoia range consists of 75 groves and covers some 35,600 acres. These groves are scattered over a 260-mile belt that is no wider than 15 miles at any one point. This narrow, scattered distribution of groves is an indication of the species' limited tolerance range in its early stages of development.

Why the scattered groves with such a broad region between the northern and southern groves where not even remnants of sequoias can be found? Did climatic changes slowly narrow and eventually disjoin a once continuous range or were there several migration routes from the various scattered regions of the east across to the Sierra's western slopes? These are just some of the many questions still to be answered. There is much conjecturing by scientists with many facts to support the rationale of the various hypotheses but as yet only the trees themselves still hold these secrets.

The hypothesis of soil moisture availability due to climatic changes is thought by many to be a major factor in sequoia distribution.

There is good evidence that approximately 8,000 years ago the climate of the earth began to warm, drying the Sierra Nevada. Due to this drying the older trees died and for the new ones survival was limited. The drier slopes became unfit for sequoia existence, shrinking their range to the present scattered groves.

The relationship between evaporation and precipitation which is caused by temperature, which in turn is increased or decreased by elevation, seems to support the widespread belief that the giant sequoia has not only stagnated but is headed for extinction. However, not all grove boundaries are shrinking, a few are slowly expanding.

The future of the entire range of the giant sequoia will depend upon climate trends and alterations by fire, man, and other disturbances. If warming and drying and the interference of man should resume, there will be little hope for our seedlings of today being seen in the year 5000.

6

Asia's Dawn Redwoods

As the Ice Age encroached and the sequoias receded to the relatively small areas that they now inhabit in California, the dawn redwood retreated to its last stand in a small region of China.

The deciduous *Metasequoia glyptostroboides* or dawn redwood grew in western North America, along with the ancestors of the two sequoias. It was this deciduous species that spread on across the northern region of the temperate zone covering what today are the frozen arctic regions. Until recent time this species was thought to be extinct; no fossils found were less than 20 million years old.

For many years redwood fossils from widely scattered regions of the Northern Hemisphere were thought to be the same as the living *Sequoia sempervirens* of the California coast region.

In 1941 Dr. Shigeru Miki, a botany professor at Osaka City

University in Japan, noticed that similar redwood fossils from Japan had an opposite arrangement of shoots, needles, and cone scales. These fossils, named *Sequoia disticha* and *Sequoia japonica*, found in rocks up to 60 million years old, had needles and shoots arranged in groups of two, opposite each other along the twigs. *Sequoia sempervirens* had needles and shoots in alternating groups along the twigs, giving a spiral effect. Another difference was the attachment of the cones at the ends of bare stalks rather than on needle-bearing twigs. These fossil cones at the ends of naked stalks had long been known from the rocks of North America, and they had been considered members of the genus *Sequoia*. Dr. Miki proposed that these two fossil species be taken out of the *Sequoia* genus and be given the new genus of *Metasequoia* to distinguish them from the true sequoias.

In 1944, T. Wang, a forester for the Ministry of Agriculture of the Chinese government, came upon a huge unfamiliar tree near the village of Mo-tao-chi in the Szechwan province in west-central China. Collecting the needles and cones, Wang then took his findings to Dr. W. C. Cheng at the National Central University in Nanking. Consultation with Dr. H. H. Hu, Director of the Fan Memorial Institute of Peking, resulted in the exciting discovery that the living tree in Mo-tao-chi was almost identical to Dr. Miki's fossil *Metasequoia*.

It meant that a tree thought to have been extinct for at least 20 million years, known only by fossils found in Japan, North America, and Manchuria, still grew in the remote area of China.

The Chinese scientists published their findings in a Chinese technical journal and sent samples to America. One of the scientists to receive the specimens was Ralph W. Chaney of the University of California. He noted that the samples bore a marked resemblance to *Metasequoia* fossils that he had found near the John Day River in Oregon. Wanting to see the living tree himself, he, along with the science editor of *The San Francisco Chronicle*, Melton Silverman, traveled to China in 1948.

Unlike the easily accessible California redwood parks, the Chinese trip proved to be a long and arduous journey. Flying to Chungking, they then took a riverboat down the Yangtze River to the town of Wanhsien, where they began a three-day walk over muddy mountainous terrain to the interior of Szechwan. On the last leg of their journey to the village of Mo-tao-chi they had to be escorted by soldiers to ward off bandits.

When they finally reached the village where the tree was discovered, they caused quite a sensation as the first white men ever seen in this remote area of China. The entire population of the valley, along with pigs, chickens, and goats, accompanied the Americans to the bank of a rice paddy to view the tree. These locals told Chaney of many more such trees growing in the neighboring province of Hupei. On seeing the trees, Chaney's belief that the fossils and living trees were indeed directly related was confirmed. The Szechwan and Hupei trees, however, did not rival their California sequoia cousins in size. The largest *Metasequoia* measured only 140 feet in height and had only a six-foot diameter, less than half the size of its California cousins. Before leaving, Chaney met with officials of the Chinese government, urging them to designate the region of dawn redwoods as a protected area. In 1965 the Chinese did establish the area as a preserve for the ancient trees and Chinese foresters propagated the *Metasequoia* in many other areas of China as well. The tree is now often used for urban planting and in certain areas of China is grown as a timber crop.

Though this was one of the most dramatic botanical discoveries of all time to scientists the world over, it was nothing exceptional to the peasants of the Szechwan and Hupei provinces where as long as anyone could remember the tree had been called the *shui-sha*, "water spruce." It grows among chestnut, oak, sassafras, sweet gum, and Katsura trees just as it did centuries ago in Oregon, Alaska, Greenland, and Spitzbergen.

Though not quite identical to Dr. Miki's fossils, the tree was nevertheless placed in the *Metasequoia* genus with a species name of *glyptostroboides*, which soon was commonly called the dawn redwood.

At the time it was discovered, it existed only in a 300-square-mile region of western-central China at altitudes of 2,100 to 4,000 feet, in a mild climate with rainfall up to 50 inches a year. Most of this rainfall is in summer. In order to survive the long dry winters, the tree is deciduous, shedding its leaves in the fall, leaving bare its ascending branches, and budding out in spring unlike its evergreen sequoia cousins.

Today the dawn redwood can be found in many parts of the

Cone and leaves of a dawn redwood

Dawn redwoods growing on the campus of the University of California at Berkeley

United States. When Chaney returned in 1949, he planted and cultivated seedlings on the campus of the University of California at Berkeley. It has since been planted in many other states. The Save-the-Redwoods League and Harvard University's Arnold Arboretum have distributed thousands of seeds and seedlings throughout England, Europe, and Asia.

The problem of survival is a difficult one and cannot be resolved without much more time and study.

Why did the dawn redwood disappear from the whole earth except in several secluded valleys of central China? We may only suppose that the combination of temperature, rainfall, and topography best suited to the growth of *Metasequoia* continued only in the Szechwan and Hupei provinces. It must also be remembered that this remote region is one of the few areas not cleared of its forests for farmland. If it were not for the remoteness of this area in central China the dawn redwoods might not have survived and we would know it only by its fossil remains. Fortunately, it was discovered before becoming extinct.

7

Man-the Exploiter

One wonders what the natural lifespan of a redwood might be. There is no known scientific reason why the redwood couldn't live forever. Seemingly immune to tree diseases, fungi, and insect attack, their fate for centuries had been accidental death from lightning fires, floods, winds, volcanoes, and earthquakes.

Then man came. Indians, trappers, farmers, miners, loggers, dairymen, fishermen, the armed forces of two world wars, armies of tourists, and finally concerned conservationists.

The footprints left by man in the redwood domain have been many and varied. Some revered the giant trees, other lived in harmony beneath them, but some destroyed them.

As far back as 2000 B.C., the first humans made their homes along the California coast among these trees. These people were the Indians of the middle and later Horizon culture, early tool-makers.

Most numerous were Yuroks, Tolowas, and Chilulas. The Yuroks settled 55 villages along the Klamath River on the California coast south of the False Klamath Cove. The Tolowas lived along the Smith River and the coast from False Klamath Cove northward. The Chilula territory was the Redwood Creek Basin.

The redwood domain provided them with timber for homes, canoes, and implements. These Indians made use mostly of fallen trees, but occasionally they would cut down a living tree.

Heated stones were pressed against one side of a tree to make a hole. Then using scrapers made of elkhorn, they would cut away the charred wood and again press the hot stones to the area. The process would be repeated higher up on the opposite side of the tree. When the tree was sufficiently weakened, gravity would finish the long and tedious task.

The tree felled, sections were then cut by the same process with heated stones and elkhorn. These rough logs were cut into planks by driving wedges of elkhorn and mussel shell into their ends. With stone adzes (primitive axes) the planks were scraped for a smooth finish.

Homes were built from these logs and planks. Log dugout canoes (18 to 42 feet long), made by the Yuroks for carrying fish and selling to other tribes, were made by the same process. The whole tree was used—log sections and cut planks, and also the bark was utilized for smaller objects such as tools, cooking implements, and

Close-up of the bark of the coast redwood. The Indians used the bark for many purposes.

even skirts made by shredding the bark. Sinkyone and Pomo Indians built their entire homes from the bark. The root fibers of the redwood were also used to weave clothes and baskets.

Redwood, combined with stone, elkhorn, or mussel shell, made excellent implements for securing food. Some tools were made to dig roots, some to harpoon seals and sea lions, and others as weapons to bring down deer and elk. These delicacies, along with shellfish, salmon, acorns, and berries from the forest environment, made for daily gourmet feasting.

The redwoods not only served the Indians' practical needs for shelter, clothing, transportation, tools, and weapons, but they served also their spiritual needs, as symbols for their religious practices and beliefs.

Similar groups of people lived in the foothills and valleys of the Sierra Nevada. The various Indian tribes of this region used the giant sequoia for practical and spiritual needs in much the same way as the coastal tribes used the coast redwood.

Some tribes such as the Miwoks had taboos against disturbing living trees, but would use the branches and bark of fallen trees for their homes and other needs.

The Mono Indians believed the trees to be sacred, not to be harmed or used at all. The spirit of the owl was thought to protect these trees and they called them Wawoma, in imitation of the owl's call. (Later, the famous Tunnel Tree in the Mariposa Grove in Yosemite became known as the Wawoma Tree. This tree was 2,200 years old. In 1881, a tunnel one could drive through was cut. This weakened the tree and it finally fell in 1969.)

In the mid-1500s, Spanish and English maritime explorers sailed past the Humboldt Coast. A few explorers even visited the area and made short journeys inland. Juan Rodríguez Cabrillo arrived in 1542, Sir Francis Drake in 1579, and Sebastián Vizcaíno in 1602. Though they wrote of California's many blessings, the redwood tree was never mentioned. It wasn't until the late 1700s that the Spanish and Russians came in any number and then only briefly stopping to trade for food and furs.

Finally, in 1768, the explorer Gaspar de Portolá was sent out from Mexico to colonize California on behalf of Spain. Several Franciscan priests accompanied him to establish missions in the newly settled lands. By October of 1769, the party had reached Monterey Bay where they came upon a remarkable grove of trees on the Pajaro River.

A priest named Juan Crespi kept the official diary for the expedition. Father Crespi entered in his diary that the Spaniards had traveled "... over plains and low hills, well forested with very high trees of a red color, of a species unknown to us. They have a very different leaf from cedars, and although the wood resembles somewhat in color, it is very different and is without a cedar odor; moreover the wood of the trees that we have found is very brittle. In this region there is great abundance of these trees and, as we know not the names of the trees, we gave them that of the color of their wood, Redwood (palo colorado) ..."

On March 26, 1776, Fray Pedro Font, the chronicler of de Anza's expedition to San Francisco Bay, recorded, "a few trees which they call redwood, a tree that is certainly beautiful; and I believe that it is very useful for its timber for it is very straight and tall ..." Three days later on their return journey, de Anza's men caught sight of "a very high redwood ... rising like a great tower." Father Font measured the tree and was awed by the proportions (though modest for a redwood) of his "palo alto" or tall tree. Today, more than a century later, the tree still stands in Palo Alto, California, which took its name from Father Font's tall tree.

The Spaniards did little harm to the "palo alto," as they preferred to build their missions and homes of adobe, or dried mud, as they had learned from the Pueblo Indians. However, recognizing the beauty and durability of the wood, they cut a few trees for the heavy beams of their larger buildings.

The Russians followed. They came in pursuit of sea otter furs and established a colony at Fort Ross on the Mendocino Coast in 1812. Only twenty-nine years later, with the sea otter near extinction, trade failures, and agricultural disappointments, the Russian-American Company of Alaska sold out and departed. All that is left of the Russian settlement are a few buildings, stockade, and chapel, all built of redwood.

In April, 1828, Jedediah Smith, a famed mountain explorer, left California's Central Valley, crossing the land with twenty men and several hundred mules and horses. He hoped by following the Trinity River to reach the Pacific. Progress was good until May 19, when, with the ocean in sight, the forest became almost impenetrable. From their camp (near what today is Orick), it took them one month to finally reach the short distance to the Klamath River, arriving June 20, 1828.

Then white man Dr. Josiah Gregg, scientist and author, tried the same trip in 1849. Underestimating the difficulty of the trip, his ten-day food supply was not adequate and he died during the expedition. However, some of his party survived to lead others into the coast redwood domain and soon boom towns began springing up along the coast.

In the autumn of 1833, between the Jedediah Smith and the Josiah Gregg inland expeditions to the coast, another explorer, Joseph Reddeford Walker, led his party across the Sierra Nevada. This expedition is credited with the first written record of the giant sequoia. Zenas Leonard, the party's chronicler, published this account in 1839 at Clearfield, Pennsylvania:

"... found some trees of the redwood species, incredibly large
—some of which would measure from 16-18 fathoms around
the trunk at the height of a large man's head from the ground."

The particular area of this discovery is not clearly documented. However, from various descriptions in the chronicle, it is thought to have been the Tuolumne or Merced Grove, both in Yosemite National Park.

Unfortunately, the printing shop in Clearfield burned to the ground. Only two copies of Leonard's narrative were saved. It wasn't until 1904, when the document was reprinted, that the world was to hear of this discovery.

Other tales of the discovery of the giant sequoias circulated before the Leonard account came to light. The first was that of A. T. Dowd.

It all began when the New York *Tribune* announced the discovery of gold in California on September 15, 1848. Gold had been found by John Marshall at Sutter's Mill in Coloma on January 24 of that year. News was slow in those days and it was nearly eight months from the time it was sent from the sleepy town of San Francisco before it reached New York.

Within a couple of years of that news, the "forty-niners" inundated this little town of less than 1,000 people. The gold rush not only changed San Francisco but the history of all California as well. By 1852, 30,000 gold seekers flooded into California annually.

New stories of gold discoveries were a daily tale in the foothill camps of the Sierras. However, in 1852, from a place called Murphy's Camp in Calaveras County, came a story of discovery of a very different nature.

While Murphy's camp was a howling success, it was in great need of water. Hence the Union Water Company was established by a group of enterprising and affluent miners.

To provide cheap food for the large number of workers on the project, the company hired four hunters. One of these was A. T. Dowd who was destined to make himself and Murphy's Camp famous over the world—and not for gold!

Dowd was an adventurer and afraid of nothing. Wandering into the heavily wooded country southeast of Murphy's Camp near the Stanislaus River, he shot and wounded a grizzly that fled deep into the forest. Dowd, following his prey intently, failed to realize at first the change in the forest's characteristics. Suddenly he found himself at the foot of a tree that stopped him in his tracks. All thoughts of hunting left him as he stared up at the wide, red trunk. Barely tapering at all, the tree rose to an incredible distance above. The first 100 feet or so were bare; the branches sprouting high above were as large as an ordinary tree.

Dowd had seen the coast redwoods, but even though taller, they seemed fragile in their slenderness compared to this graceless, red pillar.

Excitedly, he hurried back to camp to tell of his unbelievable tree. No one believed him. Some just thought it another tall story or miner's myth, popular in the camps at the time; others called him crazy or drunk.

Incensed at these implications, he decided to wait and let things die down. Then one morning after a conspicuous absence, he announced that he had shot "the largest grizzly bear that I ever saw in my life." To get the doubters into the woods, he said he needed help to get it back to camp. Dowd led them through pine groves, up steep ridges, and down canyons deep into the wilderness. At last he reached the base of the tree and, pointing, yelled, "Now boys, do you believe my big-tree story? That is the large 'grizzly' I wanted you to see. Do you still think it's a yarn?"

As far as the world then knew, this spring day in 1852, it was the first *Sequoia gigantea* seen by a group of white men. Dowd had stumbled upon what is now known as the Calaveras Grove, a part of the Calaveras Big Trees State Park, California.

Dowd's glory was short-lived. Shortly after his discovery in 1852, sightseers who came to the grove found a tree in whose bark had been carved, J. M. Wooster, June 1850. The story was investigated and it was revealed that a J. Marshall Wooster had lived at Murphy's Camp at the time. Wooster turned up to verify that he had been there with two other men but that he could not claim credit for the discovery. Two other men from Murphy's Camp set out hunting on May 20, 1850, and found the grove. He and his two friends had gone to see it twelve days later, after hearing about it. Whitehead was one of the men and the other's name he had forgotten. Thus, until 1904 when the Leonard book was reissued, Whitehead and his nameless friend were thought to be the discoverers.

By 1870, most of the larger groves of the Sierras had been discovered, extending from Tahoe National Forest, for 260 miles southward to Sequoia and Kings Canyon national parks. All are on the western slopes of the Sierra Nevada.

As the forty-niners continued to prosper, the redwoods began to decline. At first the tree was regarded with contempt because of its softness, lightness, and seeming lack of strength. Whole houses built of other woods were brought "around the Horn" to San Francisco, Oakland, and Trinidad.

Despite the early misgivings about the tree's attributes, the forty-niners eventually began to use it because it was abundant and cheap. Soon they found it had quite a lot to offer. The very qualities that saved it from nature's destruction condemned it to ruination by man. It was earth-proof, waterproof, rotpoof, termite-proof, and warp-proof. It was in demand for sawmills, homes, wagons, fences, wharfs, water tanks, barns, churches, and more sawmills.

San Francisco soon became a city of redwoods. All of the beautiful forests that had surrounded the city on the peninsula and in the East Bay hills were logged off within a decade. Now only barren, denuded forest country remained. By 1855, with no more

Early-day loggers in a coast redwood forest

nearby trees to destroy, they began cutting and shipping them in from Humboldt County.

The Humboldt coast already had been touched by the gold rush, with the presence of gold confirmed at Gold Bluffs Beach a short time before.

Not only were the trees cut for buildings for the boom towns. As time went on, many who had come only for a try at the gold began to settle permanently. Clearing the land for settling was as disastrous as logging for the forty-niners' needs. Vineyards near the Russian River, sheep meadows on the Mendocino coast, cow pastures near Scotia, Eureka, and Crescent City are still dotted with the burned-off stumps of hundreds of fallen monarchs.

A logging town in redwood country

The Pre-emption law of 1841 and the Homestead Act of 1862 only served to encourage this rape of the land. This legislation meant to benefit settlers but it proved instead to be a great boon to timber speculators and operators who were able to gain control deviously of immense tracts of public land. Even worse frauds were committed under the Timber and Stone Act of 1878. Gold seekers, merchants, and sailors were lured to the land offices where land claims were filed for them. A small wood shanty would be set up on the man's claim as the "homesteader's home." Then the "homestead" changed hands, back to the original shyster for a few dollars. Thus, some of the most valuable lands in the world passed into the hands of mostly phony "homesteaders."

The first lumbering operations were recorded in 1850. How-

*Early
logging
operations*

ever, no redwood was cut commercially in Humboldt or Del Norte counties until 1855.

It was not long before Swedes, Finns, Norwegians, Frenchmen, Germans, Englishmen, Scotsmen, and Irishmen joined American and Canadian woodsmen to pit their strength against the big trees. Thousands of board feet of redwood timber were carried to ports around the world. By the turn of the century, one logging company alone was turning out 8.5 million board feet every year, and it owned more than 8,700 acres of forest land. Thirty years later, the rate of cutting had increased to about 500 million board feet annually.

The process began with the choppers. A stage was built around the trunk of a tree at the height where it begins to narrow. Here the choppers worked with axes, saws, plates, shims, wedges, sledges, gunstocks, and a plumb bob. Felling a forest monarch, 12 feet in diameter, with these tools usually took two men three days.

The fallen giant was then cut into the needed lengths. Barkers would peel off the bark with long poles. "Jackscrewers" then rolled the peeled logs to a bull-team crew. Teams of bulls, oxen, or horses hauled the logs down the skid to the "dump" or landing at the river's edge, the string of logs bumping along behind the six-to-eight yoke of animals.

At the "dump," the jackscrewers rolled the logs into the river. Sometimes they were sent in a box flume, the naked log speedily sliding down the flume, ending in a giant splash in the river. Once in the river the logs remained until the rainy season when tumbling water would move them. The log drivers then rushed the log jam down the swollen river. Sometimes sluice dams were built to hold back a head of water and then "tripped" to release a flash flood, shooting the logs to the mill. This floating system lasted until around 1880 in Humboldt County but was successfully used until 1936 in Mendocino County.

The logs at last were ready for shipping. This was no easy process, for there were few natural harbors on this stretch of coast. Picturesque lumber schooners had to work their way through the rough coastal waters to a cove or "dog hole" to moor under a sheer cliff. Once moored, an apron chute was placed between the cliff top and the deck of the pitching ship below for loading. Sometimes the logs were lowered on swinging slings suspended from a wire cable, one end anchored to the cliff, the other on the cove bottom.

Logs that were shipped by land went by steam locomotives

Steam locomotive removes cut redwood logs from a coast forest.

dragging long strings of log-filled flatcars.

Soon another engine was to be heard in the woods, the "Dolbeer Donkey," an invention by John Dolbeer to replace the bulls and oxen for hauling. Everyone laughed at the crazy contraption—a vertical boiler, a one-cylinder engine, and a drum for winding the steel cables. However, when the contraption chugged, smoked, coughed, and gurgled, and the logs came crashing down the skid on high, no one laughed. The men had been replaced!

The redwoods continued to be cut by the thousands every year. Increasing mechanization was fast replacing the old logging methods in both the woods and the mills.

In place of the old handsaws, donkey engines, and logging railroads were gasoline-powered chain saws, crawler tractors or "cats," and huge off-highway trucks.

The first thirty years of the century had seen great progress in the logging industry and much destruction of America's coast redwood forests. Then the Depression hit and the board feet cut dropped from a 500 million annual average to a 300 million yearly average during the thirties. But with the onset of World War II, the cut accelerated and didn't stop when the war ended. It continued to accelerate until it reached one billion board feet a year by the early 1950s.

The supply of trees seemed limitless as the buzz of the chain saw, the growl of the "cats," and the frantic roar of the huge logging trucks continued year after year.

How long before the supply of ever-living redwoods would be

depleated? In one hour, man, armed with modern technology, was capable of destroying what took nature a thousand years to bring to maturity. Time was running out.

Not only the coast redwood but also the giants of the Sierra Nevada were facing a similar losing battle.

8

Man–the Protector

Once the sequoia's discovery and qualities became known, publicity was inevitable. But with publicity came destruction.

The first tree chosen for exhibition in San Francisco and later in New York was in the North Calaveras Grove. Though many seemed callous over the cutting, others were incensed. Articles from these concerned citizens expressed loathing. This was the vague beginning of a movement which eventually resulted in the public preservation of nearly all sequoia lands.

Those first protests did little to stop the destruction. A second tree, also from the North Calaveras Grove, was to be exhibited at the Crystal Palace at Sydenham, England. As the weight of the trunk's whole section would have been too heavy and cumbersome to ship, the bark was stripped to a height of 120 feet to be exhibited.

The remaining portion of the tree was left in place. With its protection gone, it lived for only a few years. The popular exhibit in England remained until fire consumed the Crystal Palace in 1966.

A third tree was cut from the Grant Grove in 1876 for Philadelphia's centennial exhibition. The remains of its trunk still lie near its more fortunate neighbor, the General Grant Tree.

In 1891, the famous Mark Twain Tree, a 331-foot-tall, nearly perfect specimen from a grove in Kings Canyon, was felled for exhibition. The base section of the trunk is in the American Museum of Natural History in New York City, the next higher section is exhibited in the British Museum of London, the rest of the tree was cut up for grape stakes and fence posts. Only the stump remains and can be seen in what is now known as Big Stump Grove in Kings Canyon National Park.

Though this exhibition cutting was reprehensible, it was only a small fraction of the destruction that was to come to the land of the giants.

Lumbering entrepreneurs were interested in much more than a few samples. Beginning in 1856, logging operations continued intermittently until the mid-1950s—100 years of destruction. The tree's low tensile strength and brittleness made it unsuitable for most structural uses. Consequently this giant of the forest was reduced to being used for such inconsequential things as grape stakes, fence posts, patio furniture, and pencils for Europe.

As lumber prices increased, more sequoias were cut. Explosives were often used which shattered much of the tree, which was then

Modern-day redwood logging

useless for harvest and the splintered debris was a constant fire hazard.

The devastation of sequoia forests was unbelievable. It will take centuries to heal the scarred land.

In Converse Basin, only one mature sequoia remains of the many thousands that once grew there. Ironically, it was the largest and was named for Frank A. Boole, Superintendent of the Converse Basin Mill, who had overseen the slaughter of the basin's 2,600 acres of sequoia.

By their last major cutting, the loggers had cut 33 percent of the original sequoia acreage.

One good thing did come out of all the devastation. Young sequoias sprouted thickly in the disturbed soils and grew rapidly.

Yosemite National Park

This cast doubts about the earlier hypothesis that the sequoia was slow-growing and on its way to extinction.

Public preservation of sequoia lands was slow in coming. In 1864, during the Lincoln administration, landmark legislation deeded the Mariposa Grove and the Yosemite Valley to the state of California. It was to be administered as part of the Yosemite grant, lands granted to California for public use, resort, and recreation to be inalienable for all time. This bill set the trend for the preservation of most sequoias.

Naturalist John Muir felt more protection was needed. He was apprehensive about the logging and grazing in the highlands above and the erosion problems related to this. Muir urged establishment of a Yosemite National Park which would include all the lands draining into the valley.

Muir's efforts and those of Robert Underwood Johnson were instrumental in the passage of further federal legislation in September of 1880. This legislation created Sequoia and General Grant national parks. Then on October 1, that same year, Yosemite Park was established.

Theodore Roosevelt fought for conservation of the redwood Calaveras Groves in the north. However, he failed to persuade Congress to appropriate the money. Finally, in 1909, a bill signed by Roosevelt created the Calaveras Big Tree National Forest. Later, in 1931, the North Calaveras Grove was added to the growing California state park system.

After many years of planning and fund raising, on September 9, 1967, both Calaveras groves were formally dedicated as part of the state park system.

In the southern Sierra in 1916, the National Geographic Society began a fund-raising campaign to purchase lands adjacent to Sequoia National Park. By 1921 the society had added 2,000 acres more of sequoias to the park.

In 1940 the last remaining large area of sequoia land, the 3,720 acres of the Redwood Mountain Grove, became Kings Canyon National Park. The bulk of the trees were now safely preserved.

Today, national parks own approximately 68 percent of sequoia acreage, national forests 21 percent, Bureau of Indian Affairs 1 percent, state and county 2 percent, and private owners 8 percent.

With sequoia logging over and parks for protection, the remaining trees appear safe for our future generations to enjoy.

The trend for "save the coast redwoods" began with an article published in *National Geographic* magazine showing the devastation of the forests. Several prominent men, appalled at the devastation, banded together in 1918 to organize the Save-the-Redwoods League. Between 1920 and 1928, the league purchased many redwood groves which formed the core of the California Redwood State Park system.

In 1928, the 9,000-acre Rockefeller Forest at Humboldt Redwoods State Park was purchased from the Pacific Lumber Company.

The Kent-Mather Grove, also in Humboldt Redwoods State Park, was purchased in 1921. In 1931, the 2,552-acre Garden Club of America Grove was purchased. Other groves bought during this early period formed the beginning of the Avenue of the Giants and the core of Humboldt Redwoods State Park.

In June, 1923, the league purchased the first redwood grove at Prairie Creek Redwoods State Park. By 1932, they had added another 5,936 acres to it. Then with matching funds from the state and league donations an additional 2,816 acres was now protected in Del Norte Coast Redwoods State Park.

Renewed interest in establishing a Redwood National Park caught on again in the 1930s. Congress again took no action. However, the league did acquire the Jedediah Smith Redwoods State Park (formerly Mill Creek State Park).

In 1949, the Public Affairs Institute of Washington, D.C.,

Dedication of Lady Bird Johnson Grove in the Redwood National Park. Speaker at the podium is former Interior Secretary Walter J. Hickel.

recommended legislation to establish a National Redwood Forest of over 2 million acres. Congress again took no action. However, Save-the-Redwoods League continued to purchase redwood lands to include in the state redwood parks.

By standing for fair compensation to those whose properties were desired for parks, the league won the respect of the lumber companies, and several of these companies cooperated by holding some of the finest forest areas until the league could raise the needed funds to buy at fair market values.

After World War II, the league continued to add to the state

Bird's-eye view of a redwood forest

parks. Again, in 1961, the idea of a National Redwood Park was revived. The National Geographic Society aided the effort by making a $64,000 grant to the National Park Service for a survey of remaining old-growth redwoods to decide on a site for the park.

Finally in 1968, after more than fifty years of trying without luck, the national park became a reality. An act of Congress to establish the Redwood National Park was signed by President Johnson.

The 30,000-acre park also was authorized to include three of the state's parks: Prairie Creek, Del Norte Coast, and Jedediah Smith, which protect the area's forest redwoods.

Ten years later, on March 27, 1978, President Jimmy Carter signed the Redwood National Park Expansion Act, increasing the park to 78,000 acres. This legislation provides for the rehabilitation of cutover lands which were included in the purchase and provision for payments to reduce the local economic impacts from these changes.

Since its founding in 1918, the Save-the-Redwood League has donated more than $37 million to protect more than 230,000 acres of coast redwood forests in 31 state parks and the Redwood National Park. The league hopes to continue to be a guardian to the big trees so as to ensure future generations their chance to glimpse these ancient monarchs of the forest.

Centuries of devastation by nature and man have come and gone, and still the redwoods stand.

To honor these monarchs, in 1980 the United Nations Educational, Scientific, and Cultural Organization (UNESCO) declared Redwood National Park a World Heritage Site. Now these great trees can take their place among other Great Wonders of the World: Australia's Great Barrier Reef, Arizona's Grand Canyon, Egypt's Great Pyramids, and now California's Trees in Trust.

Index

Page numbers in **boldface** indicate those on which illustrations appear

2-24